TAKING ACTION
TO HELP THE ENVIRONMENT

REBECCA SJONGER

Crabtree Publishing Company
www.crabtreebooks.com

UN SUSTAINABLE DEVELOPMENT GOALS

Author: Rebecca Sjonger

Series research and development:
Janine Deschenes
Reagan Miller

Editorial director:
Kathy Middleton

Editor: Janine Deschenes

Proofreader and indexer:
Wendy Scavuzzo

Design and photo research:
Katherine Berti

Print and production coordinator:
Katherine Berti

Images:

iStock
pniesen p. 5t

Shutterstock
nexus 7 p. 5b; Osugi p. 6t; dani daniar
p. 6b; JEAN-FRANCOIS Manuel p. 10b;
Maxim Blinkov p. 11; stockvideofactory
p. 16b; Holli p. 24b; Asia Images p. 25t;
Sandra Foyt p. 25 2nd from top

NASA
SRTM Team NASA/JPL/NIMA p. 9b

All other images from Shutterstock

All dollar amounts in this book are in U.S. funds, unless otherwise indicated.

Library and Archives Canada Cataloguing in Publication

Title: Taking action to help the environment / Rebecca Sjonger.
Names: Sjonger, Rebecca, author.
Description: Series statement: UN sustainable development goals | Includes index.
Identifiers: Canadiana (print) 20190134143 | Canadiana (ebook) 20190134186 |
 ISBN 9780778766643 (softcover) |
 ISBN 9780778766605 (hardcover) |
 ISBN 9781427124067 (HTML)
Subjects: LCSH: Environmentalism—Juvenile literature. | LCSH: Green movement—Juvenile
 literature. | LCSH: Environmental justice—Juvenile literature.
Classification: LCC GE195.5 .S56 2019 | DDC j363.7—dc23

Library of Congress Cataloging-in-Publication Data

Names: Sjonger, Rebecca, author.
Title: Taking action to help the environment / Rebecca Sjonger.
Description: New York : Crabtree Publishing Company, [2020] |
 Series: UN sustainable development goals | Includes index.
Identifiers: LCCN 2019023708 (print) | LCCN 2019023709 (ebook) |
 ISBN 9780778766605 (hardcover) |
 ISBN 9780778766643 (paperback) |
 ISBN 9781427124067 (ebook)
Subjects: LCSH: Environmentalism--Juvenile literature. | Sustainable development--
 Juvenile literature. | Climatic changes--Juvenile literature.
Classification: LCC GE195.5 .S59 2019 (print) | LCC GE195.5 (ebook) |
 DDC 363.7--dc23
LC record available at https://lccn.loc.gov/2019023708
LC ebook record available at https://lccn.loc.gov/2019023709

Crabtree Publishing Company

www.crabtreebooks.com   1-800-387-7650

Printed in the U.S.A./082019/CG20190712

Published in Canada
Crabtree Publishing
616 Welland Ave.
St. Catharines, Ontario
L2M 5V6

Published in the United States
Crabtree Publishing
PMB 59051
350 Fifth Avenue, 59th Floor
New York, New York 10118

Published in the United Kingdom
Crabtree Publishing
Maritime House
Basin Road North, Hove
BN41 1WR

Published in Australia
Crabtree Publishing
Unit 3–5 Currumbin Court
Capalaba
QLD 4157

CONTENTS

The Environment and the Sustainable Development Goals   4

Environmental Challenges   8

Goals to Help the Environment   14

Goal 7—Affordable and Clean Energy   15
Goal 13—Climate Action   16
Goal 14—Life Below Water   18
Goal 15—Life on Land   19

Global Collaboration   22

What Are People Doing?   24

You Can Do It!   28

Learn More   30

Glossary   31

Index   32

About the Author   32

THE ENVIRONMENT AND THE SUSTAINABLE DEVELOPMENT GOALS

The environment is the natural world in which plants, animals, and people live. Earth's many ecosystems **show how they all connect. Even the smallest change ripples through a community of living things.**

The prairies of North America are a grassland ecosystem. As they settled on the land, farmers brought farm animals with them. When farm animals started grazing there, they damaged the plants. This affected the food supply for grassland animals. Farming and many other human activities have a huge impact on ecosystems and the environment.

Grassland plants and animals thrive in dry, windy conditions.

Most of North America's grasslands are used for farming. Due in part to the damage farming causes, they are one of the world's most endangered ecosystems.

THE GREAT BARRIER REEF

Coral reefs are marine ecosystems. One-quarter of ocean plants and animals live in them. Australia's Great Barrier Reef is Earth's largest coral reef. It is 3,000 times bigger than Disney World in Florida! More than 1,500 species of plants and animals live there, and close to two million people visit the Great Barrier Reef each year. More than 60,000 people have jobs that depend on it. They work in a wide variety of areas, including tourism, fishing, and science.

The Great Barrier Reef and everything that depends on it are in danger. Rising water temperatures and pollution are major threats. One of the many harmful effects is **coral bleaching**. It can kill coral, which leads to habitat loss for other marine life. High water temperatures wiped out about one-third of this reef in 2016. Half of it is now dead. *National Geographic* compared the event to a forest fire. People are taking action to save the reef that remains. For example, some groups are trying to improve the water quality. Others aim to protect local wildlife or restore bleached coral.

The Great Barrier Reef is Earth's largest living structure. But human activity is threatening its survival.

THE UNITED NATIONS

The Great Barrier Reef is just one of many ecosystems that need help. Protecting the environment is one of the missions of the United Nations (UN). Its members are from 193 countries. **Sustainable** development is at the heart of their global efforts. This kind of development meets today's needs without harming the ability to meet the needs of the future.

The UN also promotes peace and human rights worldwide.

UNITED NATIONS NATIONS UNIES

5

2030 AGENDA
FOR SUSTAINABLE DEVELOPMENT

In September 2015, more than 150 international leaders met at the UN's headquarters in New York City. They approved an action plan to help people around the world thrive. It also looks after the planet for future generations. They called it the 2030 Agenda for Sustainable Development. By that year, it aims to:

- **Improve people's lives through better jobs, health care, and education**

- **End poverty**

- **Increase** economic growth

- **Reduce** climate change **and protect people from its impact**

The flags of member countries fly outside of the UN headquarters in New York City.

Flooding in Jakarta, Indonesia is a common threat. People living in poverty feel the effects the most. They may be unable to afford to move to safer areas, repair damage, or replace belongings.

SOCIAL INEQUALITY

The UN is also trying to reduce social inequality. This can happen when some people have fewer opportunities and less power and money than others. They are more at risk when an unplanned event, such as a natural disaster, occurs. **Vulnerable** people include children, the elderly, pregnant women, people who are ill, and those living in poverty. Everyone feels the impacts of environmental issues. However, social inequality places vulnerable people in greater danger.

AN UNFAIR WORLD

Outdoor air pollution is one example of social inequality. More than half of it is created by the richest 10 percent of the world's population. For example, they may often travel by airplane, which causes a lot of pollution. Outdoor air pollution causes health problems, such as lung cancer, and kills more than three million people each year. People living in poverty are most at risk of dying because of it. Wealthier people can usually avoid living in places with the highest pollution levels. Look at your community. Who lives closest to the factories, highways, and dumps?

GOALS THAT WORK TOGETHER

The UN's 2030 agenda focuses on 17 Sustainable Development Goals (SDGs). They were launched on January 1, 2016. Each goal fits together with the other goals. For example, taking care of the environment helps promote things like good health and clean water. To be sustainable, the SDGs balance economic growth, the environment, and social issues. This book focuses on how Goals 7, 13, 14, and 15 help the environment. To see how these goals fit together and shape a better world, flip to page 14.

TEAMWORK MAKES THE DREAM WORK

People around the planet are collaborating, or working together, to reach the goals. Youth play a big part in hitting the UN's goals. When you are an adult in 2030, what kind of world do you want to live in? You can play a role in shaping the future!

ENVIRONMENTAL CHALLENGES

Earth's climate changes naturally over time. In the past, these long-term weather patterns shifted very slowly. Human actions over the past two centuries sped up these changes. They also became more hazardous. Today's climate change includes higher temperatures, rising global sea level, decreasing sea ice, and more extreme weather. These have major impacts on living things worldwide.

GLOBAL WARMING

The rising temperature of Earth's **atmosphere** is called global warming. The release of **carbon dioxide** and other gases are mostly to blame. They are known as greenhouse gases. **Emissions** of these gases trap heat in the atmosphere. Burning **fossil fuels** such as coal, gas, and oil is the main source of greenhouse gases. China gives off more emissions than any other country. However, Americans and Canadians give off highest emissions per person. If action is not taken, the global temperature will continue to rise. It could go up by 2.7°F (1.5°C) or more in the next decade or two. This is enough to destroy or harm many ecosystems and living things.

Carbon dioxide emissions have gone up over 50 percent since 2000. Average temperatures worldwide rose about 1.8 °F (1°C) between 1880 and 2017.

RISING SEA LEVEL

Global warming melts land-based ice such as glaciers and **ice sheets**. The water flows into the oceans. This raises the sea level. Higher temperatures also affect the sea level. Warm ocean water takes up more space than cool water does. From 1901 to 2010, the average global sea level rose by 7.5 inches (19 cm). It could rise up to 30 inches (76 cm) or more by 2100. This would flood coastal cities, from India's Mumbai to New York City. Millions of people might lose their homes and ways of life.

As sea levels rise, waves reach further onto land. They erode, or wear away, the land, damaging the roads and buildings on it.

PREDICTING THE FUTURE

By how much will the sea level rise in the future? Making predictions is difficult. The Intergovernmental Panel on Climate Change (IPCC) and the National Oceanic and Atmospheric Administration (NOAA) have different sea level forecasts for 2100. The numbers change depending on the expected levels of greenhouse gases.

2100 SEA LEVEL FORECASTS

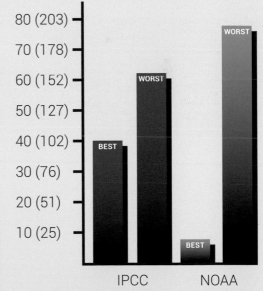

BEST CASE TO WORST CASE AVERAGE INCREASES, IN INCHES (CM)

80 (203)	
70 (178)	WORST
60 (152)	WORST
50 (127)	
40 (102)	BEST
30 (76)	
20 (51)	
10 (25)	BEST

IPCC   NOAA

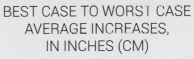

? Which American state will be helped the most if we can stop the sea level from rising?

Answer: Florida—most of the top 25 American cities at greatest risk are there

9

MELTING SEA ICE

Every summer, some of the ice on the Arctic and Antarctic oceans melts. It freezes again when winter arrives. The thickest ice does not melt completely. It is called multi-year ice and it is more common in the Arctic. This sea ice is a habitat for animals such as polar bears and seals. In the past, multi-year ice made up about half of the ice in the Arctic Ocean. About 95 percent of it has disappeared since 1985. This polar region could be completely ice-free for part of the year by 2100—or sooner. Without a permanent ice cover, the dark ocean water **absorbs** more sunlight. This causes even more ice to melt and raises global temperatures.

Polar bears hunt on the sea ice. As it disappears, they must walk great distances to reach ice. Many are starving.

DANGEROUS WEATHER

Extreme weather events such as droughts and floods are severe and hard to predict. They are becoming more common because of climate change. These events are more destructive than ever. For example, Hurricane Maria devastated Puerto Rico in 2017. The next year, a heat wave broke records around the world. More than a million people in Malawi, Mozambique, and Zimbabwe were affected by flooding after Cyclone Idai in 2019. Vulnerable people have the most difficult time bouncing back when extreme weather hits.

This Puerto Rican child stands in his destroyed neighborhood. His family and many others did not have resources to rebuild their lives after Hurricane Maria.

Oceans cover three-quarters of the world's surface. Plastic waste is a huge water pollution problem.

IMPACTS ON OCEANS

Earth's oceans help make the planet livable for humans. They have a huge impact on the global climate and water cycle. They also hold food sources, **biofuels**, and medicines. More than one billion people depend on ocean-based foods, and millions of people have jobs in marine industries. But these industries, as well as other human activities, cause many problems. Overfishing and water pollution are major issues. Carbon dioxide also harms the oceans. The water absorbs the emissions, which causes it to become more **acidic**. Ocean acidity hurts marine life—harming ecosystems and depleting human food sources. For example, shelled animals such as oysters cannot form properly. Acidity has gone up about 26 percent with the rise of industries. Changes to coastal ecosystems also cause issues during extreme weather. Coastal areas provide natural barriers against storm damage. Without them, extreme weather may cause more harm.

Deforestation happens when widespread areas of trees are cut down. There is a lot of deforestation in the Amazon rain forest.

DEFORESTATION

More than one-third of Earth's land is covered in diverse forests, from rain forests to **boreal forests**. Wooded areas are habitats for 80 percent of land-based plants and animals. They also provide food, homes, and livelihoods for some **Indigenous** populations. Forests are in trouble worldwide. Deforestation is a big issue. More than 30 million acres (12 million hectares) of woodlands are cut down each year. Trees help prevent global warming by absorbing carbon dioxide. Without them, more gases go into Earth's atmosphere.

DAMAGED LAND

Deforestation can damage the soil, meaning that it is less able to grow plants. This is called land degradation. Pollution, farming, and extreme weather such as drought also cause it. In some cases, desertification occurs. This turns land into a sandy desert. Because of desertification, the Sahara Desert has grown by about 10 percent in the last century. Land degradation affects many poor people worldwide. More than half of the land used by farmers has been spoiled.

LOSS OF LIFE

Threats such as deforestation and land degradation lead to the loss of many kinds of plants and animals. About eight percent of known animal species are already extinct. More than 20 percent are now at risk for extinction. Many at-risk animals are illegally hunted and sold. This issue affects humans, too. For example, 75 percent of major medicines come from plants. Species could disappear from the planet without us ever knowing how they could have helped people.

Forests can be used for recreation, which promotes well-being (Goal 3).

Affordable, clean energy is targeted in Goal 7. Reaching it will help reach other goals too, such as sustainable cities and communities (Goal 11).

ENERGY EFFECTS

Why have people done things that harm the environment? At first, we did not know better. As scientists study Earth, we learn more about how we can help or hurt it. For example, our energy sources have had a big impact. Burning fossil fuels is the main cause of the current climate change crisis. We now know they make up more than half of greenhouse gases. The UN's goal is to cut worldwide emissions by 45 percent by 2030. They hope to end emissions completely by 2050. The solution lies in switching to clean, renewable energy sources that do not pollute or run out. Solar, water, or wind power are all good options. Energy must also be affordable and available to all people. This is the best way to stop global warming and it helps meet many other goals.

TARGETING ENVIRONMENTAL ISSUES

Environmental issues affect everyone. But poor and vulnerable people are usually hit the hardest. Making sure no one is left behind is a core mission of the SDGs. Helping the environment plays a huge part in building a world in which people are equal. The SDGs that focus on climate, life on land and in the oceans, and energy all fit together. They also relate to other goals. Goals 3 and 15 connect because plant-based medicines can help achieve good health. Land degradation (Goal 15) must be stopped to end hunger, since farmers need good soil to grow food (Goal 2). Achieving the UN's environmental goals helps reach other goals, too.

GOALS TO HELP THE ENVIRONMENT

The Sustainable Development Goals fit together to form an action plan. Each of the 17 goals has its own targets. They focus on the main causes of the issue. A goal is achieved when all its targets are hit.

Within each target are one or more indicators. They are measurable ways to track if progress is being made. Each connected part comes together like a blueprint.

GOAL

7 AFFORDABLE AND CLEAN ENERGY

TARGET

Make sure that everyone has access to modern energy that they can count on and afford

INDICATORS

Increase in the number of people around the world who have electricity, and who rely mainly on clean fuel and technology

If the numbers in this example drop enough, the target will be hit. This shows progress being made toward meeting the overall goal.

7 AFFORDABLE AND CLEAN ENERGY

Air pollution from burning wood and coal indoors caused 4.3 million deaths in 2012.

AFFORDABLE AND CLEAN ENERGY

About one billion people around the world cannot access electricity. It is needed to meet basic needs, such as refrigerating food and medicine or running a water pump. Without electricity, they must burn coal and wood to cook and heat their homes. The smoke can make them seriously ill. African countries are the most affected by the lack of clean energy. The targets of this SDG fight these inequalities. One aims to increase the amount of renewable energy used worldwide. It is measured by the amount of renewable power used compared to other, less modern sources. Another target aims to improve global collaboration and **investment** that relates to research, technology, and clean-energy systems. Its progress will be shown by an increase in the amount of money spent on these programs.

CHALLENGES TO OVERCOME

Burning coal is the greatest source of carbon dioxide emissions. Despite the clear link between fossil fuels and global warming, people are burning more coal than ever before. There are also millions more gasoline-burning cars on the road each year—creating more emissions. That is because transportation needs are growing along with the world's population. Providing affordable and clean energy in **developing countries** and war zones is especially difficult.

GLOBAL EFFORTS NEEDED

Goal 7 can be reached by:

- **Creating clean and renewable energy solutions that are inexpensive and dependable**

- **Planning for mass transit such as trains instead of using cars**

- **Urging wealthier countries to help developing regions**

Building renewable energy sources is essential. But in dangerous areas, such as war zones, builders may not be able to construct them.

13 CLIMATE ACTION

As oceans become warmer, hurricanes become stronger.

CLIMATE ACTION

Tackling climate change is a big task! We need to do all we can to stop global warming, the rising sea level, melting sea ice, and worsening extreme weather. A key target is making sure every country is fighting climate change. The first step and a major indicator is whether they have a national plan. We also need to raise awareness of climate change and how to reduce it. This can be measured in part by the number of countries that are educating their citizens about climate change. Another target is for UN members to donate to the Green Climate Fund. This fund helps developing countries address climate change. The hope is that $100 billion will be given each year by 2020.

GLOBAL EFFORTS NEEDED

This goal could be met if we:

- **Build up low-carbon industries that use clean technologies**

- **Invest in renewable energy sources (see Goal 7)**

- **Encourage worldwide support of the Paris Agreement, which deals with greenhouse gas emissions**

Low-carbon industries are those that do not put out many greenhouse gas emissions. Industries can become low-carbon by using renewable and clean energy sources.

Many people use gasoline for transportation, or rely on energy from fossil fuels to light and heat their homes. It can cost money or require a lifestyle change to switch to renewable energy sources.

CHALLENGES TO OVERCOME

Most climate change issues are getting worse instead of better. Weather patterns keep changing. Extreme weather events can throw people into poverty without warning. They hurt the local **economy**, cause hunger, and damage people's health and well-being. Greenhouse gas emissions are at their highest level ever. Most of the Arctic's multi-year sea ice is gone. Some areas of the planet are already threatened by the rising sea level. Caribbean islands are losing coastlines, for example. One-quarter of St. Kitts and Nevis are already under water!

THINK DEEP

How have you seen climate change treated in the media?

What do you notice about how political leaders talk about climate change?

Is there anyone who benefits from this goal not being met?

Marine animals can become tangled in trash or try to eat it.

LIFE BELOW WATER

A simple way to help life below the water is to stop polluting. Preventing and reducing water pollution is a target the UN wants to meet by 2025. Seeing how much plastic trash is in the oceans is one indicator. Another big target is lowering and repairing ocean acidification. Progress will be measured by how acidic the water is. Controlling fishing and ending overfishing will also help marine life. Numbers of fish will show if this target is met. The UN also aims to protect at least 10 percent of the world's coastal and marine areas. Counting the number of protected areas is a key indicator.

CHALLENGES TO OVERCOME

A major challenge with Goal 14 is getting people to care about it. When asked, many leaders thought it was the least important SDG. This is despite the fact that huge patches of garbage swirl around on the world's oceans. Trash extends from the surface down to the depths, threatening marine animals. Living things in oceans are also in danger if acidification continues. It is important to educate ourselves and others on how ocean health affects all life on Earth.

GLOBAL EFFORTS NEEDED

People can hit these targets by:

- **Stopping plastic waste from reaching the oceans**

- **Supporting the UN Convention on the Law of the Sea, which directs how countries around the world use oceans**

- **Increasing awareness of what is happening in oceans**

THINK DEEP

What could happen if one Sustainable Development Goal is ignored?

How does this impact the other goals?

15 LIFE ON LAND

Due to soil erosion, few plants are able to grow in this region of Senegal.

LIFE ON LAND

A lot needs to be done around the world to help life on land. One huge target focuses on forests. It includes managing them well, stopping deforestation, helping damaged forests, and planting new trees. The UN's goal is to see progress being made in all these areas by 2020. It also wants to fight desertification, restore damaged land, and make land use sustainable. Progress will be made if the amounts of degraded land decrease. Another target looks after protected plants and animals by stopping the theft and sale of them. Counting the amount of wildlife that is sold illegally shows if this is being achieved.

CHALLENGES TO OVERCOME

Deforestation and land degradation harm Earth's air quality, animal habitats, and food sources. Over 2.5 billion people depend on farming to survive. They need healthy soil on which to grow crops and raise animals. However, degradation has spoiled over half of the world's farmland. This issue needs to be addressed to avoid global hunger.

GLOBAL EFFORTS NEEDED

What can the world do?

- **Focus on reforestation, or the planting of trees**

- **Protect animal habitats and tree species**

- **Find ways to fight desertification and improve farmland**

- **End the sale of endangered species**

Kids Saving the Rainforest rescues sick and hurt animals and helps return them to the forest.

YOUTH FOR
CHANGE

When Janine Licare was nine years old, she and a friend, Aislin Livingstone, wanted to save their local rain forest in Costa Rica. They also wanted to help the animals living in it. The girls raised money by making and selling bracelets and other crafts. Janine's mom helped them buy four acres (1.6 hectares) of rain forest. Over time, it became an 82-acre (33-hectare) wildlife rescue center! The organization has spread to 18 other countries. It collaborates with other groups to help with reforestation and animal protection.

ORGANIZATION	Kids Saving the Rainforest
ESTABLISHED	1999
ORIGIN	Manuel Antonio, Costa Rica
FOCUS	Protecting rain forest plants and animals
INVOLVEMENT	Collaborates with schools, scientists, and volunteers from around the world

Rain forests have a huge diversity of plant and animal species.

? What percentage of tree species have been studied for uses such as medicines?

Answer: Only one percent!

Countries make plans to help citizens affected by natural disasters. This British rescue team offers help to those affected by a flood.

GOALS FOR GOOD

Meeting the targets for one goal helps us work toward others. For example, one of the targets of Climate Action (Goal 13) is helping people affected by natural and climate-related disasters. Making plans to reduce the risks is a big part of this. If successful, it will also help with the global goals that focus on vulnerable people, such as No Poverty (Goal 1) and Good Health and Well-Being (Goal 3). Each one of these goals must be met to create a sustainable world. Every effort has a wider impact!

One target aims to help people protect themselves against natural disasters, such as by using sandbags to stop water.

GLOBAL
COLLABORATION

We need worldwide efforts to achieve the Sustainable Development Goals. Leaders agreeing to them at the UN was just the beginning. Everyone must collaborate to put these plans into action. Youth can take the lead! They are our future change-makers and innovators.

BETTER TOGETHER

Most people and groups have their own special interests or areas of focus. Great things can happen when they work together! They can share ideas and points of view. Collaborators can also put their resources together. This means more skills, knowledge, tools, time, and money are available. They can accomplish much more together than they could working on their own.

A BIG TEAM

All member nations of the UN are working together to meet the SDGs. This includes the poorest to the wealthiest nations on Earth. Each country also has its own plans related to the commitments it has made. They need widespread participation to be successful. All of us, from kids in schools to leaders at all levels of government, need to do our part. Civil society organizations (CSOs) bring together people with a shared interest in helping the public. They do not make a profit and are not run by governments. Businesses also play an important role in achieving the SDGs.

Greenpreneurs participants hold climate action workshops to help develop their ideas together.

PARTNERS FOR PROGRESS

Youth Climate Lab is a great example of collaboration. It brings together students, CSOs, businesses, and governments. This youth-centered network was started in 2017. Recent university graduates Dominique Souris and Ana González Guerrero wanted to get young people involved in environmental policy and projects. Youth Climate Lab has become a hub of creative ideas and innovation. Its 2030 Lab Series engaged youth in learning about the SDGs. They thought of creative policy recommendations, researched solutions, and shared ideas. Another one of its projects is Greenpreneurs. It is a partnership with Global Green Growth Institute and Student Energy that brings together teams of young innovators. They help develop their energy, water, forestry, farming, and green city ideas.

THINK DEEP

Are you already part of a club or team that could take action to help the environment? If so, which steps could you take to get started?

How could you inform people in your school or community about the SDGs?

WHAT ARE PEOPLE DOING?

There is no time to waste in working toward the Sustainable Development Goals. Global citizens are already tackling many environmental issues.

Global citizens are people who understand how world issues affect us all. They collaborate with others in their communities and around the globe. Every effort gets us closer to meeting the goals. They also help create a fairer, more sustainable world.

YOUTH FOR CHANGE

When Greta Thunberg was 15 years old she started skipping school on Fridays. She headed to the Swedish government buildings with a sign. It read *Skolstrejk För Klimatet* (School Strike For Climate). Students around the world followed her lead. More than one million youth strikers have demanded climate action. Thanks to Greta, global leaders are paying attention to the demands of these young people.

ORGANIZATION	#FridaysForFuture youth strikes
ESTABLISHED	August 20, 2018
ORIGIN	Stockholm, Sweden
FOCUS	Inspiring students worldwide to fight climate change
INVOLVEMENT	Young people in over 70 countries—and counting!

Thousands of Australian students gathered for this climate change strike in November 2018. Thousands more have participated in strikes since then.

MARK YOUR CALENDAR

The UN and many other organizations attract attention to important issues through global action days. These special events take place on the same day each year. They may include community projects, education, and fundraising efforts. Here are just a few examples:

APRIL 22
EARTH DAY

About one billion people celebrate with one-day projects such as neighborhood cleanups and tree planting. Each year has a different theme. It was End Plastic Pollution in 2018 and Protect Our Species in 2019, for example.

MAY 17
ENDANGERED SPECIES DAY

A spotlight is placed on animals and plants that may disappear from Earth forever. Events include youth art contests, adopt-an-animal fundraisers, and education programs.

JUNE 8
WORLD OCEANS DAY

This day hosts worldwide events to help our oceans. They include fundraisers, educational programs, and trash collecting on beaches.

DECEMBER 14
WORLD ENERGY CONSERVATION DAY

Celebrated in more than 5,000 cities, this day focuses on innovative, renewable energy sources. People are also urged to reduce their energy use.

YEAR-ROUND HELP

You do not have to wait until a specific day to take action! There are many ways to get involved throughout the year. Projects such as Plant-for-the-Planet's Trillion Tree Campaign and many others present creative solutions. There is something for every age, interest, and skill level! For example, the zero-waste movement encourages people to create as little garbage as possible. Individuals, groups, and communities around the world have taken up the challenge. They might only buy products that come without packaging. Or they could choose foods and items that will get used up. Sometimes, collecting information is the first step in meeting a goal. Earth Challenge 2020 is a collaboration in which people from around the world answer six questions. The topics range from plastic waste to local air quality. This data helps them plan and carry out ways to help the environment.

SOCIAL ENTREPRENEURS

Young change-makers can start their own businesses that also help solve social issues. These social enterprises provide decent work and economic growth, which helps meet Goal 8. They can also address a variety of SDGs. For example, LiveGreen in Europe puts on events such as music festivals and fashion shows. They are designed to provide lifestyle ideas to help fight climate change. Businesses can balance making money and helping the environment!

The University of Waterloo's Affordable Energy for Humanity Global Change Initiative aims to create affordable energy technologies and services. They want to make sure all people can use clean energy.

THINK DEEP

Global change starts at the local level. Who makes important decisions in your own community?

How could you contact leaders to tell them about the kind of world you want to live in?

It is estimated that Americans use more than 500 million plastic straws every day. Many of them end up in the world's oceans.

YOUTH FOR CHANGE

Nine-year-old Milo Cress saw that restaurants gave customers plastic straws without asking if they wanted them. He was concerned about all of the unnecessary plastic waste they created. So he raised the issue with some local businesses. Milo convinced them to ask people if they wanted straws instead of giving them out every time. His goal was to reduce waste. However, his campaign sparked something much bigger. People around the world are now looking for ways to replace single-use plastic items, such as straws.

ORGANIZATION	Be Straw Free campaign
ESTABLISHED	2011
ORIGIN	Burlington, Vermont
FOCUS	Global awareness of single-use plastic products
INVOLVEMENT	Widespread international participation

Are any restaurants in your community offering alternatives to single-use plastic items?

YOU CAN DO IT!

Today's generation of youth is the largest ever. There are almost two billion young people on the planet! Each one could be a powerful change-maker. By working together, this group can save the world. Are you ready to take action?

REFLECT

- What could the world look like in 2030 if the Sustainable Development Goals are achieved? What if they are not?

- Are you interested in any of the people, groups, or projects you read about in this book? Find out more about them!

- How could you help the environment in your own community? Are there natural areas or animals that need protection? How could you get more information?

- What skills or abilities do you have to offer?

ACTION PLAN

Just like the UN created the 2030 Agenda for Sustainable Development, you can make your own action plan. Helping the environment begins with steps like the ones listed below. What is one action you could take today?

7 AFFORDABLE AND CLEAN ENERGY	• Use power bars that can be turned off when not using the items plugged into them • Research how you could use renewable energy at home or at school instead of older sources
13 CLIMATE ACTION	• Encourage your family and friends to live sustainably now instead of waiting until it's too late • Reduce your carbon footprint by taking public transportation, biking, or walking
14 LIFE BELOW WATER	• Buy ocean-friendly foods and products • Find reusable options to replace single-use plastic items • Hold a clean-up day in a coastal area
15 LIFE ON LAND	• Limit the amount of trash you make and recycle whatever you can • Plant trees • Eat local, sustainable foods

FUTURE GOALS

Helping the environment and working toward the UN's other goals does not end in 2030. Worldwide efforts must be ongoing. The SDGs follow in the footsteps of the Millennium Development Goals. These eight goals were **enacted** in 2000. They focused on poverty, education, social equality, health, the environment, and global partnerships. They helped shaped the later SDGs. Progress will need to be kept up if the current goals succeed. If there is still more work to be done, today's youth will be the leaders who decide on the next steps.

LEARN MORE

WEBSITES

Brush up on your climate knowledge:
https://climatekids.nasa.gov

Find out more about saving Earth's oceans:
https://on.natgeo.com/2WRpAJ4

Explore how the World Wildlife Fund is helping save the planet: **www.worldwildlife.org**

Learn about all the Sustainable Development Goals: **www.youneedtoknow.ch**

FURTHER READING

Bradman, Tony, editor. *Under the Weather: Stories About Climate Change*. Frances Lincoln Children's Books, 2012.

Kurlansky, Mark. *World Without Fish*. Workman Publishing, 2014.

Weyn, Suzanne. *Empty*. Scholastic, 2012.

ACTIVITIES

Check out the ideas at Change for Climate:
https://changeforclimate.ca/action

Explore and play on the Government of Canada's Climate Kids site:
https://climatekids.ca

See how you can celebrate Earth Day:
www.earthday.org/earthday

Play the Go Goals! board game found at
https://go-goals.org

Try one of the 170 daily actions to transform our world at **https://bit.ly/2LGK9Un**

GLOSSARY

absorbs Takes in or soaks up

acidic Describes a substance that contains acid and has a PH lower than 7. PH is the measure of acid in a substance. Pure water has a PH of 7.

atmosphere The gases surrounding Earth or other planets

biofuels Fuels, or sources of energy, that are made from living things. Wood is one example.

boreal forests Forests that grow in Earth's northern hemisphere and are mostly made up of coniferous trees, such as evergreen and pine trees

carbon dioxide An invisible gas that is produced by burning fossil fuels and traps heat in the atmosphere

climate change The gradual change in Earth's usual weather. Usually refers to global warming, or the gradual increase in Earth's average temperature, caused by human activity.

coral bleaching The process by which coral whitens, caused by it losing its algae. Often caused by an increase in seawater temperature or acidification.

developing countries Countries with fewer industries and a lower Human Development Index, which measures such things as life expectancy, income, and education

economic growth An increase in the number of goods made and services provided

economy The system of how goods are produced, bought, and sold

ecosystem An interconnected community of living things that depend on each other, as well as the nonliving things in their environment

emissions The discharge, or sending out, of a substance

enacted Put something into action

fossil fuels Natural fuels, or sources of energy, that come from plants and animals that died long ago

hazardous Dangerous or risky

ice sheets A permanent layer of ice that covers a large area of land

Indigenous A broad term that describes groups or nations of people who are native to an area

investment The act of giving resources to a cause to help in its success

sustainable Able to continue for a long time because it does not cause damage to people or the environment

vulnerable More likely to experience harm

INDEX

#FridaysForFuture 24

2030 Agenda for Sustainable Development 6

acidic water 11, 18
affordable energy 13, 15, 26
Affordable Energy for Humanity Global Change Initiative 26
African countries 15
air pollution 7, 15
Americans 8
at-risk animals 10, 11, 12, 18, 19, 20, 25
average temperatures 8

Be Straw Free 27

Canadians 8
carbon dioxide emissions 8, 11, 12, 15, 16
China 8
civil society organizations (CSOs) 22, 23
clean energy 13, 15, 16, 26
climate change 6, 8, 9, 10, 13, 16–17, 24, 26
coal burning 8, 15
coastal areas 9, 11, 17, 18, 29
collaboration 7, 22–29
coral bleaching 5
Cress, Milo 27
Cyclone Idai 10

deforestation 12, 19
desertification 12, 19

Earth Challenge 2020 26
Earth Day 25
Endangered Species Day 25
extreme weather 8, 10, 11, 12, 16, 17

farming 4, 12, 13, 19, 23
flooding 6, 9, 10, 21
fossil fuels 8, 13, 15, 17

global citizens 24
global efforts 5, 15, 16, 18, 19
Global Green Growth Institute 23
global warming 8–10, 12, 13, 15
goals 7, 12, 13, 14–21, 29
grassland ecosystem 4
Great Barrier Reef 5
Green Climate Fund 16
greenhouse gas emissions 8, 17
Greenpreneurs 23
Guerrero, Ana González 23

human activities 4, 5, 8, 11, 13
Hurricane Maria 10

illegal hunting 12, 19
indicators 14, 16, 18

Kids Saving the Rainforest 20

land degradation 4, 12, 13, 19
Licare, Janine 20
LiveGreen 26
Livingstone, Aislin 20
low-carbon industries 16

marine life 5, 11, 18
Millennium Development Goals 29

natural disasters 6, 10, 21

oceans 5, 9, 10, 11, 13, 16, 18, 25, 27, 29
overfishing 11, 18

Paris Agreement 16
plant protection 19, 25
Plant-for-the-Planet 26
planting trees 19, 25, 26, 29
plastic straws 27
plastic waste 11, 18, 25, 26, 27
polar bears 10
pollution 5, 7, 11, 12, 13, 15, 18, 25
poverty 6, 7, 17, 21, 29
Puerto Rico 10

questions 9, 20

rain forests 12, 20
reforestation 19, 26

renewable energy sources 13, 15, 16, 17, 25, 29

Sahara Desert 12
sea ice, melting 8, 10, 16, 17
sea level, rising 8, 9, 16, 17
single-use plastic products 27, 29
social enterprises 26
social inequality 6, 7, 29
soil erosion 9, 19
Souris, Dominique 23
Student Energy 23

targets 13, 14, 15, 16, 18, 19, 21
Think Deep 17, 18, 23
Thunberg, Greta 24

UN Convention on the Law of the Sea 18
United Nations 5
United States 8, 9

vulnerable people 6, 10, 13, 21

water pollution 5, 11, 18, 25
working together 7, 22–29
World Energy Conservation Day 25
World Oceans Day 25

Youth Climate Lab 23
youth strikers 24

zero-waste movement 26

ABOUT THE AUTHOR

Rebecca Sjonger is the author of more than 50 books for young people. She recommends the many resources created by the United Nations. They are a great starting point to learn more about the Sustainable Development Goals!